Dinosaurs

Brachiosaurus

Daniel Nunn

Heinemann
LIBRARY

www.heinemann.co.uk/library
Visit our website to find out more information about Heinemann Library books.

To order:
 Phone 44 (0) 1865 888066
Send a fax to 44 (0) 1865 314091
 Visit the Heinemann Bookshop at www.heinemann.co.uk/library to browse our
catalogue and order online.

First published in Great Britain by Heinemann Library,
Halley Court, Jordan Hill, Oxford OX2 8EJ, part of Harcourt
Education. Heinemann is a registered trademark of Harcourt
Education Ltd.

Editorial: Daniel Nunn and Rachel Howells
Illustrations: James Field of Simon Girling and Associates
Design: Joanna Hinton-Malivoire
Picture research: Erica Newbery
Production: Duncan Gilbert

Printed and bound in China by South China
Printing Co. Ltd.

10-digit ISBN 0 431 1845 0 X
13-digit ISBN 978 0 4311 8450 0

11 10 09 08 07
10 9 8 7 6 5 4 3 2 1

British Library Cataloguing in Publication Data
Nunn, Daniel
Brachiosaurus. – (Dinosaurs)
567.9'12
A full catalogue record for this book is available from the
British Library

Acknowledgements
The publishers would like to thank the following for permission
to reproduce photographs: Alamy pp. 6, 10 and 23 (Mike
Danton), 22 (www.white-windmill.co.uk); Corbis pp. 7
(Galen Rowell), 12 (Jim Zuckerman), 22 (Louie Psihoyos);
Getty images pp. 18 (National Geographic/Maria Stenzel),
19 (Science Faction/Louie Psihoyos), 20 and 23 (The Image
Bank/Grant Faint), 21 (News/Cancan Chu).

Cover photograph of Brachiosaurus reproduced with
permission of Corbis/Jim Zuckerman.

Every effort has been made to contact copyright holders
of any material reproduced in this book. Any omissions will
be rectified in subsequent printings if notice is given to the
publishers.

Contents

The dinosaurs 4

Brachiosaurus 8

How do we know?. 18

Fossil quiz 22

Picture glossary 23

Index 24

Notes 24

The dinosaurs

Dinosaurs were reptiles.

Dinosaurs lived long ago.

Brachiosaurus was a dinosaur.
Brachiosaurus lived long ago.

Today there are no Brachiosaurus.

Brachiosaurus

Compsognathus

Some dinosaurs were small.

But Brachiosaurus was very big.

Brachiosaurus had long legs.

Brachiosaurus walked slowly.

Brachiosaurus had a very long neck.

Brachiosaurus could eat the leaves at the top of trees.

Brachiosaurus ate plants.

Brachiosaurus ate stones, too!

Sometimes, other dinosaurs
attacked Brachiosaurus.

Brachiosaurus used its feet to fight back.

How do we know?

Scientists have found fossils
of Brachiosaurus.

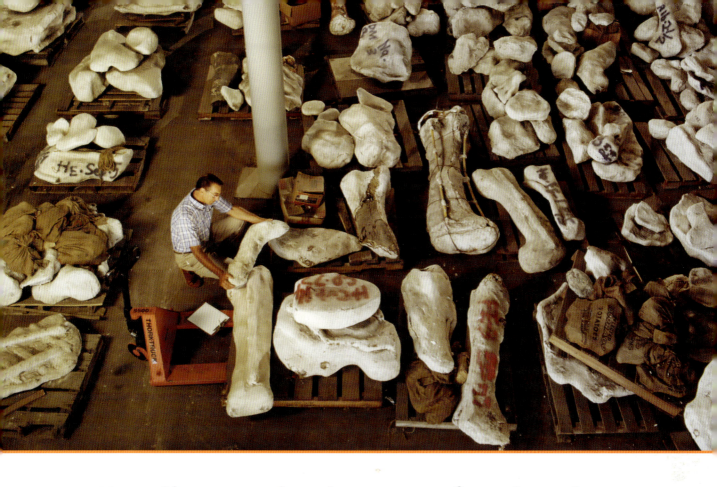

Fossils are the bones of animals which have turned to rock.

fossil

Fossils show us the outline
of the dinosaur.

Fossils tell us what
Brachiosaurus was like.

Fossil quiz

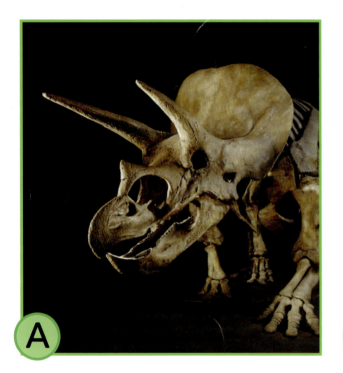

A

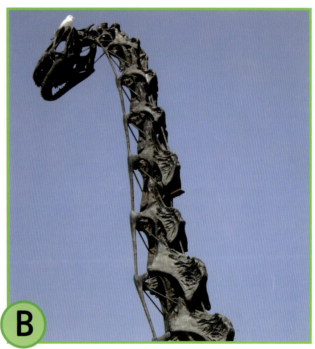

B

One of these fossils was Brachiosaurus. Can you tell which one?

Picture glossary

dinosaur a reptile who lived millions of years ago

fossil part of a dead plant or animal that has become hard like rock

reptile a cold-blooded animal

Answer to question on page 22
Fossil B was Brachiosaurus. Fossil A was Triceratops.

Index

fossils 18, 19, 20, 21, 22

reptile 4

scientists 18

Notes to Parents and Teachers
Before reading
Talk to the children about dinosaurs. Do they know the names of any dinosaurs?
What features did they have e.g. long neck, bony plates, sharp teeth? Has anyone
seen a dinosaur fossil or model in a museum?

After reading
• Sing a Dinosaur song to the tune of 'London Bridge is falling down'.
  Dinosaurs lived long ago, long ago, long ago.
  Dinosaurs lived long ago
  Now they are extinct.
  Continue with e.g. Brachiosaurus had a very long neck/ Brachiosaurus ate plants
  and stones etc.
• Read a dinosaur story e.g. *Dinosaur Roar* by Paul and Henrietta Strickland
• Make a Brachiosaurus collage. Draw a large outline of a Brachiosaurus and help
  the children cover the body using scrunched tissue paper etc.

Titles in the *Dinosaurs* series include:

Hardback   978-0431184500

Hardback   978-0431184517

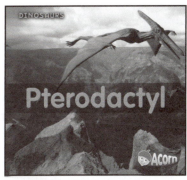

Hardback   978-0431184494

Hardback   978-0431184470

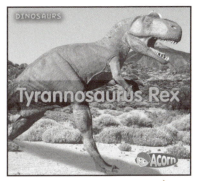

Hardback   978-0431184463

Hardback   978-0431184487

Find out about other titles from Heinemann Library on our website www.heinemann.co.uk/library